DEMOCRACY IN AMERICA

SARDONIC SPECULATIONS

Paul N. Goldstene

Three Essays with
a Postscript on
Equal Opportunity

Davis, California 1988

1st Printing February 1988
2nd Printing November 1988

Bucknell House
1214 Bucknell Drive, Davis, California 95616

Table of Contents

Judicial Review as "Democratic" Ideology (1977) **5**

American Democracy
The Crucial Contradiction (1978) **33**

Theft as the Basis of American Public Policy
An Instructive Instance (1985) **45**

House of Forty Thieves
Or The Limits of Equal Opportunity (1983) **59**

Judicial Review as "Democratic" Ideology
(1977)

It is a very dangerous doctrine to consider the judges as the ultimate arbiters of all constitutional questions. . . . The Constitution has erected no such single tribunal, knowing that to whatever hands confided, with the corruptions of time and party, its members would become despots.

Thomas Jefferson

Judicial Review as "Democratic" Ideology

American politics form a strange configuration. Populated by liberals who think they are democrats, the nation is, in fact, happily dominated by an institution which represents historical tribute to the assured dogma of conservative imagination. Thus does rule prevail. Thus is reality hidden. From the perspective of those anxious to run things, all in America is as it should be.

This is a condition that begins with popular sovereignty. The notion, invariably mouthed, endlessly admired, rarely understood, that an abstraction known as "the people" is the necessary source of all authority which might be claimed by an apparatus considered to be a government, is the starting point of all political discourse in America. Only a government of this kind is a real government. Only it can command loyalty. All else is the pretension of power, and power commands nothing but revulsion and revolution.

Such an abstraction is, in itself, not democracy, although there exists no shortage of this delusion. Neither is it liberalism—nor conservatism. In political form, it is nothing. But in political sentiment, it is a great deal. Popular sovereignty becomes the pervasive *Grundnorm* of modern politics and, given the political history of man, a rather healthy one, at least from the point of view of those not in charge and who look to some conception of human limitation on the authority of the state.

In the hands of the most successful of American political thinkers, popular sovereignty leads to the United States Constitution, and it is the Constitution which becomes the leitmotif of American ideology, and which must be understood in its own terms if the current reality of the American system is to be comprehended. Within every nuance and dimension, the Constitution expresses an attempt to prevent what its writers most fear—the emergence of democratic rule. On the foundation of popular sovereignty, the framers of the Constitution construct an order safely guarded against government by the incompetent who, it is abundantly self-evident, are most people.

For Madison and his compatriots in Philadelphia, "the many" is a nasty formulation, worse even than "faction," and categorically frightful when combined with that dire possibility. Although the propaganda of the war against Britain had emanated from the thoughts of Jefferson and Paine, and attention to "the people" was, as a result, politically required, great care was taken that such attention did not extend beyond the first few words of the Preamble. Nothing is worse than rule by the majority faction, a concoction which must yield the tyranny of the many, wherein the tyrants, deficient in rational capacity, and unduly subject to the demands of the appetites and the passions, are so plentiful in number as to comprise a condition that is beyond the capability of sensible men to allow. In a regard for their own liberty, the people must be protected from themselves. The Constitution must become what it does become, an elaborate attempt to render political equality impossible, and it must do this in the name of the sovereign people who are rational enough to know they are not rational enough to rule.

The fear of mass rule was nothing unique, or even new, despite pressures for popular government in a proportion never before confronted. What makes the Constitution historically significant is that it represents more than this. Those who devise its stipulations are not merely antidemocrats, they are liberal antidemocrats. That they do not trust majorities is plain. That they do not trust anyone else, including themselves, is less plain, but ultimately more important. The nature of all previous governments is factional control, and the nature of factional control is tyranny. The tyrannies of the faction of the one, the few, or the many are all possibilities; all are repugnant and, given the history of the human personality, which is dual in its essential characteristics, and within which the passions persistently threaten to subvert the workings of the reason, the emergence of one tyrannical form or another is all too probable, and the emergence of the tyranny of the many is even more so.

Regardless of the enormous differences in rational capacity between the few and the many, between the members of a qualified elite—those who transform their inherently superior rational capacity into an immediate ability—and the average person, the natural disposition of all who possess authority is tyranny. Whether of the dictator, the oligarchy, or the mob, each is destructive of liberty, especially that liberty which derives from individual property ownership. In the realm of liberty, no government can be trusted. Yet the definition and protection of liberty, the translation of natural rights into civil liberties and civil rights, makes the state an unfortunate necessity. That governments only become operational when they are run by human beings, and the assumption that no human beings, no matter how superior their capacity for reason, and how advanced the development of that capacity, can be trusted with the authority of the state, are the formulating elements of the liberal dilemma. For the writers of the Constitution, the problem becomes one of instituting a government run by an elite that cannot be trusted, and the constraints of the constitutional idea alone are not enough to satisfy the insistent demands of liberal perception.

Still, among those present at Philadelphia, there are people who have no problem trusting themselves, and others sufficiently like themselves. These men adopt the contention which is the foundation of the conservative tradition since Plato and before, the contention of a supremely qualified elite that need not be guarded against. Indeed, in this view, all that can check the elite are people who, by natural definition, are less than elite, and to seriously entertain such nonsense is self-evident confirmation of common status. Within this argument, the abiding epistemology of the conservative tradition of Europe becomes decidedly American through the premise that the necessary attribute of those who are proper rulers is not superior feeling or intuition, but an unusual quantity, and even quality, of the inner reason.

Herein is the position of Hamilton, Randolph, and Marshall. But those of their persuasion lose the battles at Philadelphia to the forces of Madison and, importantly, to the implicit threat of a Jeffersonian veto which appears a not unlikely outcome of the ratification process. For the conservatives, as well as, finally, for the liberals, the democratic pretensions of the War for Independence are coming home to roost. Out of the jumbled claims and counterclaims of the independence movement, which somehow insist that the people are the political sovereign, also devolves the idea that state governments are legal sovereigns that can be dictated to by none but the people within their several jurisdictions. Accordingly, the ratification procedure, as all else in early American politics since the injection of Locke into the New World must, reluctantly, find its final justification in a state by state conception of popular sovereignty.

With the victory of Adams and Madison, the Constitution becomes a liberal triumph. Its complex arrangement of ordered liberty discovers its inspiration in the very terms of the liberal dilemma, a view of man which affirms that only the few are qualified to rule, and which is equally certain that these few are categorically unworthy of political trust. But, to define rights and protect them, to transform rights from a philosophic abstraction into a reality of human existence, a certain risk need be taken. Government is necessary, and the elite must rule, its members cloaked with the authority of the public offices which they will occupy. This is to be done in accord with the republican principle, wherein authority is conceived of as vesting in the office, not in men, who are separate of it, and who are accountable for personal actions which cannot be immunized by the screen of an authority that is, by definition, beyond prosecution. The holder of the office must, in some way, be elected to it by others, and is allowed to wield the specified political authority of the office only for a delineated, and preferably short, tenure. For the liberals at Philadelphia, the lessons of history dictate distrust.

Yet, to the minds that produce the Constitution, the danger to liberty remains enormous and unacceptable. It must be mitigated by the contractual relationships among those offices which comprise the functional authority of the state. For this reason, authority is separated into four operative departments, the executive, the judicial, the Senate, and the House wherein, following Plato, one is grounded in the form of monarchy and the virtue of honor, two are based on the form of aristocracy and the virtue of moderation, and one is predicated on the form of democracy and the virtue of equality. They are then set in opposition by being partially reconnected, a contrivance—with particular attention being paid to assuring that the probable excesses of a democratic House will be immediately controlled by an aristocratic Senate—which yields part of the checking apparatus for which the Constitution is known.

This, along with the division of authority between general and state governments, results in a distribution of authority among fourteen legal sovereigns within two divided and contending systems, producing fifty-six agencies of government, many arrayed against each other, and all of which, if executed properly, eventuates in a mechanical tension of systemic balance. In its structure, the Constitution represents an attempt to avert tyranny through the establishment of a "dynamic equilibrium"; a condition that quivers but does not go anywhere, which creaks and groans but remains essentially the same; a commitment to the status quo that students of politics now typify as an order of "competing elites." The entirety is subsumed within the overriding constraints which are the very purpose of a constitution, the notion of the revocable authority of a state that is limited to the expressed stipulations of the contract, stipulations that can never be ascertained by the state itself. A felt need for government, and a reflexive wariness of those who will run it, yields the United States Constitution, a formulation which ramifies from the liberal commitment to popular sovereignty, but which is not the only possible doctrinal consequence of that ubiquitous pronouncement.

All of this is obvious. However, within the presumed constitutionalism of modern America, there exists a wondrous world of doublethink, an arena wherein shared illusion and empirical reality are categorically distinct, wherein logic is suspended as an archaic annoyance not deserving of serious consideration. Cynicism in politics is a product of being lied to by others frequently and on a regular basis. But those who lie about the fundamental character of the American system do so most effectively to themselves. Hence, in America, there are few cynics and many enthusiasts. The lie in which the nation most cogently indulges, and which dominates the mind of American politics by controlling its pivotal conceptions and language, is that there is a Constitution when, in reality, throughout most of American history, none exists.

As certain as Madison is that the inclination toward faction will destroy the constitutional configuration, as sure as Adams is that the passions of man will subvert the Newtonian Constitution so carefully wrought by the most advanced of human reason, each conceive that the structure they inspire will survive a generation. That both these dour philosophers are not dour enough is tribute to the internal delicacy of a political order that reflects the intricate requirements of the liberal perspective.

The Constitution prevails for fourteen years, exhausting its noble effort in 1803. With the institution of judicial review as the official doctrine of the United States Supreme Court, and with the successful infusion of this doctrine into American ideology and politics, the constitutional experiment culminates in historic failure. What Marshall propounds in *Marbury* v. *Madison* is a new system, a system of "effective," as opposed to constitutional, government. Yet the terms of the debate established at Philadelphia need to be respected. The Constitution must be abolished in the name of preserving it, and in the name of the will of the sovereign people which creates it.

At issue in *Marbury* v. *Madison* is the nature of the federal union, whether the American order is to be unitary, a confederation, or patterned on the federalism of Madison and, in fact, of the Constitution, a conception which attempts to avoid the dangers and exploit the advantages of each of the others. Beyond this lurks the need of some, including the Court, to determine which agency of what government shall, under the unitary system actually being promulgated, regulate the developing contours of American politics. Needless to say, Marshall will not talk about the political issues, as he also will not really talk about the content of the case. Setting the format for subsequent judicial history in the America that follows, he prefers to talk about the Constitution.

In the Judiciary Act of 1789, Marshall expounds, Congress conveys to the Supreme Court authority to issue writs of mandamus in cases that originate in that Court, and it is on this basis that Marbury et al. postulate their suit. But the authority of the Supreme Court is enunciated in Article III of the Constitution and, while the authority for mandamus in cases on appeal is found therein, the authority to issue writs of mandamus in cases of original jurisdiction is not. Clearly, Marshall contends—behold the lawyer who employs "clearly," "therefore," or "thus," the shell game is on—clearly, if the writers of the Constitution intended this authority for the Court, they would have said so. Since they did not say so, this was not their intention.

Under the doctrine of constitutional supremacy, Marshall continues, a law not pursuant to the higher law cannot be a law. Section Thirteen, Clause C, of the Judiciary Act is repugnant to Article III of the United States Constitution and is, therefore, null and void and not enforceable in the courts of the United States. That which Congress so generously bestowed cannot, in all gratitude and humility, be accepted by this Court because to do so would be to comply with an action which is "unconstitutional."

Madison plainly knew that, beneath the guise of constitutional supremacy, Marshall had abolished the Constitution. Nonetheless, given the situation, there was no way to politically react. Marshall had proceeded with an acumen worthy of the best of Machiavelli. By instructing Madison that Marbury deserves his commission, and then claiming that the Constitution prohibits the Court from issuing a writ ordering the Secretary of State to deliver it, because the law which creates such authority is unconstitutional, the Marshall Court usurps the American system—not through a coup d'état, that is too simple—but through a fundamental revolution in political substance and form.

The selection of mandamus in original cases as the legal foundation upon which to destroy the Constitution is a tribute to the political genius of Marshall, and as about as uncalculated as the result, and as the fact that it is Marshall, as Secretary of State under Adams, who "forgets" to deliver the commission to Marbury in the first place. It is on the basis of such a triviality that one system of government is abolished and a new one brought into existence. If the historical consequence is unplanned, its correspondence to the doctrine of the Hamiltonian wing of the Federalist Party, within which Marshall was a major figure, is one of those amazing coincidences about which succeeding generations are at least entitled to wonder.

It is precisely because no one cares about the legal point that Marshall is able to win the political point with an absolute minimum of disruption. Marshall does not even afford Madison the courtesy of ordering the commission delivered to Marbury, whereupon Madison can refuse and thereby embarrass a judiciary already wanting in public esteem. With little furor, indeed, the Marshall Court ensures that Madison is immobilized on the immediate issue of the case and, more important, on the greater issue of the actual composition of the union. If Madison now awards the commission to Marbury, that will be a generous, but private, act. If, as expected, he does not, then he will fulfill Marshall's personal, and publicly proclaimed, view regarding his fundamental lack of decency. It matters not at all. The hands of the Court are tied by its stated obligation to the Constitution.

Judicial review has arrived, and the Court's authority to employ mandamus in cases of original jurisdiction is not exactly a consideration which will catapult the forces of constitutionalism into fervent and frenzied opposition. Marshall surrenders mandamus in cases of original jurisdiction. In exchange, as history will slowly make clear, he gains the Constitution. All the opposition can do is hope that judicial review will atrophy from disuse, but this is not to be. Jefferson, a democrat who comes to embrace the liberal Constitution as the best chance of restraining a government which must become tyrannical, because the empire over which it has jurisdiction is so vast that the general government must become removed from any semblance of popular control, will note that after the decision in *Marbury* v. *Madison* every ruling of the Supreme Court comprises a constitutional convention. This, of course, is precisely the point. For constitutionalists, the will of the sovereign people has been stolen. But for Marshall, it has merely been placed in the proper hands.

As is well known, the authority of judicial review is not found in the Constitution, but rather in the dicta with which Marshall precedes his own opinion, and it is the substance of these dicta which achieve an alien yet pervading acceptance in the ideology of an otherwise liberal people. The judges, Marshall declares, are the guardians of the Constitution, defending it against violations by the Congress, however inadvertent such violations may be. Inferentially, the Court must equally protect the Constitution against errors of the President, although this is not mentioned by a politically shrewd Marshall, because it was Washington who signed the Judiciary Act and, along with it, the unconstitutional section and clause, into law, and the continued popularity of Washington is a phenomenon not to be ignored. The Court is reluctantly forced into this role, Marshall explains, because its members take a solemn oath to support and defend the Constitution of the United States, suggesting that Congress and the President do not or, since they do, that, in some mystical sense, the oath of the Court is of a higher and more binding order than the oath of those in other departments of government.

All courts, Marshall proceeds, hearing a case, must put a construction on the law. "Therefore," the highest court must put a construction on the higher law or, more plainly, on the Constitution. To assert that the transition from judicial construction to judicial review represents a difference only in degree and not in kind, is to employ analogy to move from truth to falsehood. What the assertion avoids, as it must avoid, is that law is a product of government, that government is a product of the Constitution, and that law and constitutional law differ not in quantity, but in the intrinsic qualities of what they are. It also denies the glaring fact that the Court is an agency of the state, and that what Marshall is really proposing, with great historical success, is that a particular agency of government possesses the authority to interpret the will of that which has created it, the will of the sovereign people, of which the Constitution is a fundamental expression.

There is no evidence that Marshall finds any audacity in this remarkable claim. For him it is self-evident that there exists an elite which, by virtue of an inborn superiority of reason, and through the proper development of this natural capacity, is most capable of comprehending the laws of nature and, thereby, the rational, the true, and the moral which, by accepted assumption, are each part of the other and, in their totality, are that of which natural law consists. It is equally self-evident that beyond this elite there exists a supreme elite, those combining innate talent with judicial temperament and training, and who, apparently not subject to the influence of the emotions are, among the qualified, the most qualified to determine matters of rationality, truth, and morality, to determine, that is, justice and, hence, the conclusive concerns of constitutionality. Because it is but a dictate of reason that a progressive understanding of natural law must be incorporated into the constitutions and governments of man, and that this is the desire of the sovereign people, those best able to perceive the laws of nature are those best able to rule. In a rational order, that which "is" instructs what "ought" to be. The paramount judicial elite not only can rule, it should.

What results is a historic love affair with the Supreme Court, the guardians sitting high on the mountain, undoubtedly Mount Olympus, plucking down the natural truths of the universe and translating these truths into the binding proclamations of constitutional law. There is, to be sure, a cloud cover between those on the Court and all others of the human species, lesser elite and otherwise, who, unable to penetrate the concealing mist, cannot exactly perceive what it is the Court does. Yet, as the Wizard of Oz well understood, incomprehensibility is necessary, and duly admired as long as Toto does not pull on the curtain. Apparently, in America, Toto does not. At least since the Civil War, the institution of judicial review is not even questioned. Objections do develop to particular justices, but these simply reveal the suspicion that a wrong priest has attained the bench, and it is the pretender, not the priesthood, which demands remedy. Even the assault on the Court in the 1950's was against Earl Warren, never against judicial review.

It is the dicta of *Marbury* v. *Madison* which precisely illuminates the essential distinction between the constitutional supremacy of Madison and the judicial supremacy of Marshall although, in the American tradition, the supremacy of the judiciary is characteristically defended in terms of protecting the supremacy of the Constitution. Within a constitutional system any agency of any government is subject to the plenary control of the contract which creates the state. The authority and, as a consequence, the existence, of any instance of government is thus subject to the will of a human force that surpasses it, a force that composes the very mechanism of limitation. It follows that any legal sovereign, a government which cannot be legitimately dictated to by any other government, can always be legitimately dictated to, and even abolished, by that which created it, the political sovereign which, in the constitutional formulation, is the people. The political sovereign may delegate all the authority it naturally contains, and reserve none, an unlikely event in the tradition of constitutional expression. Yet it always maintains control over the state which it wills into existence because it cannot delegate away its own sovereignty or, in Lockian terms, the sovereign people cannot delegate rights which, by definition, are inalienable and, among these rights, the right to revolution is self-evident and invariable.

Now, however, one agency of one of the several governments established by the Constitution, becomes unrestrained and unlimited except, in the dubious language of Frankfurter, through "judicial self-restraint," a tacit admission that, constitutionally, there is no restraint. But this arrangement of authority is not compatible with a constitutional order. It represents, instead, a judicial oligarchy or, at best, and as Marshall was certain it would, rule by a judicial aristocracy.

Gone is the elaboration of separation and checks so carefully wrought, and which renders the Constitution a tribute to the liberal imagination. Also gone is the division of authority, the federalism which eventuates in two autonomous and balanced systems of legal sovereigns, since a Court which guards against constitutional violations by the general government must, by inference, also guard against possible incursions by governments of states, an inference that, sixteen years later, *McCulloch* v. *Maryland* will make clear. The controlling conceptions within the

Constitution derive from the specific delegations of authority it enunciates, delegations beyond the ability of any governmental agency to change or regulate. But, with the imposition of judicial review, the authority of every public office in the United States comes under the suzerainty of the United States Supreme Court which, accordingly, defines its own authority as well.

Following *Marbury* v. *Madison*, a new political order materializes in America. The sovereign people, in constitutional fact, if not in general belief, now delegate all its authority into the Supreme Court which, in turn, and as it sees fit, distributes the authority of the various agencies of the various governments that constitute the enormous complexity of the American system. In contemporary America, this reality is eagerly accepted. One thing that is not on everyone's political lips is judicial review, its position so entrenched it is no longer thought about. Most people are content with the view that the Constitution provides for it or, for the more sophisticated, intended it, although its vast usurpation of authority actually comprises a revolution in the actualities of American politics. There is no longer a Constitution. There is, however, a Court.

The conservatives at Philadelphia did attempt to write a review agency into the Constitution, a Court of Revision to be made up of the Supreme Court and the President. But to preserve constitutional supremacy, Madison finally argues, no agency of government can be allowed to interpret the Constitution, because that agency which interprets becomes supreme and where an agency of the state is supreme the Constitution is not. Governmental review and constitutional government are in essential conflict with each other. The only permissible interpreter is that whose will the Constitution is, the sovereign people of the several states. Thus does the cumbersome apparatus of the amending article, however fictional its alleged relationship to the will of the people, and replete with the liberal penchant for checked elites, become a tribute to the idea of constitutional supremacy and, not surprisingly, the only method provided to constitutionally change the Constitution. Despite the much vaunted "flexibility" of the document, the Constitution is highly inflexible, changeable through no procedure other than that which Article V provides, and even this is constrained in regard to a federal prohibition of the slave trade and federal implementation of anything other than per-capita taxation, at least before 1808, as well as in reference to the basis of representation in the United States Senate. The real flexibility of the Constitution is achieved only when the Constitution is discarded. What then emerges is a "Constitution" that is totally flexible because it does not exist.

A Court now interprets a supposed Constitution which, it must be remembered, is the expressed will of the sovereign people. The Court is the final enunciator of that will. In the conventional wisdom, the people remain sovereign. But the government they bring into existence has clearly escaped sovereign control.

All of which raises serious questions about the alleged sovereignty of the people. Some years ago Dick Tracy confronted his new nemesis, a character known as "Mumbles." Surrounded by his mob, Mumbles would periodically issue orders which were patently binding on those he led. But Mumbles could not be understood. All he could do was mumble. When he did, one of those around him would inevitably ask, "What did Mumbles say?" With equal inevitability, someone else would inform the others what it was that Mumbles said, an authorized command which, with great dispatch, was carried out.

What Mumbles actually said can, of course, never be known. All that is ascertainable is what his interpreter, however inexplicably selected, says he said. Whose will dominates? Who is sovereign, Mumbles or the interpreter? The people mumble and the Court, possessing the last word on the subject about which they presumably mumbled, tells them not only what they said, but also what they intended and, indeed, if they actually mumbled at all.

An interesting system. But not one which can be categorized as constitutional, because the interpreter is an agency of the state and, in regard to that agency, there is no constitutional restraint.

If Dick Tracy is too prosaic, there is always Hitler. The controlling will of the Reich is the blood genius of the Aryan race, the modern form of the archaic notion of *das Volk* or, in more familiar terms, the sovereign people. This controlling will resides most perfectly in the person of the Fuhrer, whose expression of it accords it direction and is the concrete realization of its mission in history. Without this articulation by the Fuhrer, the sovereign will remains horde-like and historically aimless. In the unlikely event that disagreement develops between the paramount leader and *das Volk* as to what the will of the people is, the Fuhrer, through his elite genius for intuitive understanding, is always correct.

Although the contentions of the Nazis are rooted in a Romantic "theory" of knowledge, whereas the epistemology which grounds judicial review emanates from Rationalism, the analogy is sound. The rampant elitism of the Nazi position is blatant. To the American mind, the rampant elitism of judicial review is less so. Strangely, those who are egalitarian in other matters, seem to lose their political bearings when it comes to the Court. Yet, a system wherein the Fuhrer interprets the will of the Aryan race, and a system wherein the Supreme Court interprets the will of the sovereign people are, in grandiose presumption and interior logic, identical. Within each there exist gradations of elites, with the elite of elites performing the crucial function of interpreting the ruling dictates of the sovereign will. Whenever the Fuhrer determines—whenever the Court decides—a convention of a self-authorizing elite has occurred. If the analog of Nazism is disturbing, the fascists are available. The claim is the same.

It is because claims of this type are not empirically defensible that Madison argues for constitutional supremacy. If disagreement occurs about what the will of the sovereign people is, let every jurisdiction, as they ramify from the separation and division of authority, proceed according to the views of those who currently hold these various offices. In short, let there be politics. If confusion must be resolved, the people can always do so through the amending process. While confusion is not always desirable, a certain amount is certainly preferable to tyranny. Herein is the price—if it is a price—of constitutional government.

A state is constitutional or it is not. It is restrained by a human force beyond government, or it is not. The political purpose of the philosophical construct known as the sovereign people is, plainly, to establish the aggregate of the population as a constraining force. When the people are effectively co-opted by the government, the government, inescapably, becomes authoritarian, since it is no longer constitutional and, with the exclusion of anarchy, there exists no other possibility. Hence, in the name of the Constitution, an authoritarian system comes to be insinuated into America.

But logic does not end here. Judicial review produces an order wherein one agency of the state defines the authority of all other agencies and, most important, its own authority as well. Because a definition of authority is, in fact, a delegation, that which finally determines authority is, in fact, the political sovereign. Or, when that which is limited stipulates its own limitations, there is no limit. The legal sovereign and the political sovereign are one. The state becomes the source of its own authority, a de facto inference of all authoritarian formulation in the history of political thought. Under the doctrine of judicial review, the legal sovereign or, more accurately, one agency of the several legal sovereigns that the Constitution creates, is actually transformed into the political sovereign. Not only does that which was constitutional become authoritarian, but the sovereign people are abolished as a political force.

Logic notwithstanding, it remains a general American conviction that the United States is a constitutional system, and that the review function of the Supreme Court works to keep it so.

"If no one is above the law, then the law itself is supreme."[1] Within this archetypical expression of the accepted ideology lurks the notion that America is a nation of laws, not of men, a notion reassuringly reiterated in introductory textbooks and, with sophisticated fervor, by pundits learned in the subject. It implies that the law is subject to the Constitution. But the Court absorbs this arcane conception. As Chief Justice Hughes, in a moment of unguarded honesty, notes, the Constitution is what the Court says it is or, more directly, the Court is the Constitution, as well as the law that is supposedly pursuant to it.

The political intention of the constitutional perspective is central to the Lockian contract. This is a contract between the sovereign people, or Dr. Frankenstein, the superior party, and the state, for all liberals the monster, and clearly conceived of as the inferior party. The premise of the contract is that the monster can never get loose because it is always dissolvable by Dr. Frankenstein through the fundamental act of revoking the contract. Indeed, the sovereign ability to do so is exactly what defines the superior party to the agreement.

But now the monster is loose, unnoticed in its domination of the order because it has assumed the cloak of the contract itself. Among the influential, it is increasingly popular to blame the vast problems of American public policy on the "fact" that "democracy" has gone too far, that people in general do not possess the political capacity necessary to deal with the enormous difficulties of the twentieth century, that what is most required is the benevolent guidance of the qualified few. This is not exactly a new idea. But few notice that this is precisely what exists, that people in general have nothing to do with policy, that, in terms of constitutional law, the people in general have been constitutionally dissolved.

All this may be beneficial, and those closest to the judicial vocation are reassuring on the point. Legal scholars approximate near universality in pointing out that judicial review is a pivotal safeguard against the tyrannical dispositions of the majority. The very idea of a Constitution "turns on the concept that governmental action may be unjust even if willed by most of the people" and that, in the United States, judicial review devolves from "the . . . practical dilemma involved in finding means to constrain a majority to a course it finds distasteful. Our thought is devoted to devising mechanisms of government—presently our Supreme Court—which can defer the effectiveness of hasty, intemperate, and arbitrary acts of rule until they are replaced by more settled and more just policy."[2]

This is a view that is accorded great and learned respect. Certainly Marshall must applaud its assumption that most people are intemperate and not to be trusted, and that only a wisdom which emanates from judges can yield a reasoned result. It is a position, popular in America, deriving from the proposition that, in one way or another, the majority literally rules, or threatens to, a proposition which is empirical nonsense. But the thrust of the position goes further. It equally denies the value of factional conflict and the pluralistic configuration of competing elites which the Constitution intricately mandates. Only the American analog of the Philosopher King, those who populate the judicial department, released from even the implicit constrictions of the republican principle regarding a circumscribed term of office, are capable of discerning the much-desired general welfare.

In America, any acclaim for conservative rule is most effectively formulated in the classical liberal terms of the protection and improvement of natural rights. But, aside from the unique episode of the Warren Court, nothing in judicial history supports this contention, except for the judicially protected rights of the few who enjoy the appropriate relationships to productive property. As Burke would have it, all are equal in their possession of rights, but what they have a right to is not the same. Those who struggle to extend the reach of liberty, and to equalize the conception of who is entitled to it, typically derive from elsewhere in the American system. There are judges who have championed an equality of rights—usually a minority on the Supreme Court—but history is far more generous in offering examples of members of the judicial department as caught by the reactionary hysteria of the moment as those who elitists habitually portray as the eminently impressionable "masses."

There is no evidence that democracy, which is as unchecked and authoritarian as judicial supremacy, and which, in any event, never applies to America, or to any other nation-state, would be less amenable to individual liberty than the current system. The same is true of an actual constitutional government. "If one defines 'constitutional justice' as that condition in which citizens may trust their government to uphold certain rights considered inviolable, it is clear that judicial review of statutes is only one way of attaining this happy state. In fact, in a given country political factors may perhaps provide a better check than the courts on attempts to establish majoritarian tyranny."[3]

Separate of the inference that courts are not "political," Madison would agree. Liberty for Madison is only possible where there is constitutional supremacy, and where the tyrannical disposition of each faction is countervailed by the similar disposition of opposing factions. The essential protection and promotion of liberty is found not in courts, but in the proper organization of power and authority. If, for practical reasons, a final interpreter of the Constitution is required, a consideration Madison never really allows, let it be the most popular department of government, wherein the plurality of factional contention is best reflected, not that agency most removed from the competition of interests. Moreover, as with the British, let no elitist claim to ultimate interpretation attend the fact of interpretation.

This, of course, is a proposal which is highly unacceptable to the American people who are deeply enamored of the absolute necessity of judicial review and who direct to its institutional formulation an enormous degree of psychological authority. But a people so enamored cannot be democrats. More relevant to the American experience, they cannot even be liberals who, after all, trust no one with unrestrained authority. What is remarkable is that a people who pride themselves on their democratic commitments, and who, in conflict with this, are liberals who deeply distrust not only majority authority, but authority of any kind, have thoroughly digested the conservative dicta of *Marbury* v. *Madison*, transforming it into a central ingredient of their ideology and political self-conception. This can only be accomplished when the Court is perceived, as Marshall would have it perceived, as existing above politics. Yet Americans are, in the final analysis, liberals who do comprehend the judicial function as "above" politics and, accordingly, above the probability of tyranny, a comprehension based on a conditioned distinction between "mere" matters of "politics" and "fundamental" matters of "constitutionality."

The impact of judicial review on the operative process of American government is plain. But its consistent purpose may have less to do with claims about competence and the enhancement of liberty and the attainment of justice than with financial and technological considerations. It could be, as Marshall strongly felt, that judicial review is required because the Constitution is too cumbersome and constraining to promote the manifest destiny of the American economic empire. If the historical meaning of a nation is colonial and imperial, power and authority must be concentrated, not pluralized. If the Newtonian atomization of authority and the checking apparatus which characterize the Constitution work against concentration, such an order must be abolished and the system brought into line with the conglomerated unity of the national will. The significance for policy is profound. The causal relationship between the Taney decision in the *Dred Scott* case and the end of any chance of Congress averting the Civil War is instructive. So is the successful interference of the Court with the New Deal, a success that materialized from a general acceptance of the propriety of judicial review, and without which the economic programs of the Roosevelt administration might have worked, and the subsequent dependence of American business on war and war preparations avoided. Nonetheless, throughout the 1930's, while people starved, they applauded the Court as it employed its self-proclaimed authority to discover the true principles of economics, much as it did in the late nineteenth and early twentieth centuries in reaction against earlier efforts to render wealth distribution more equal. It effectively persisted, as attempts to influence its real power, even within the parameters of judicial review, were labeled as "Court packing" and dismissed as a "political" campaign to sabotage the stipulated demands of the Constitution itself.

In their politics, Americans are liberals. But the delusion, grounded in a salient liberal distrust of politicians, that constitutional law is a realm separate from politics, permeates. Thus, in reference to the Constitution, Americans are unwitting conservatives, impervious to their immersion in contradictory ideologies, and to the understanding that an order wherein the "political" is controlled by the "constitutional" is authoritarian when ruled by an elite which has taken charge of the Constitution. In an immediate sense, other forces have clear policy importance in America. However, over any substantial period of time, the Court prevails. It picks its cases and establishes the public agenda, and those privy to the conceptions and language which emanate from the presiding influence of judicial review, and through which the population is manipulated, those trained in the law, come to define the style and substance of the national experience. As judicial review becomes entrenched and unquestioned, the formulation and implementation of policy more insistently takes place in a greater variety of courts, those agencies of the state which are most removed from popular or factional control, a condition which demands an increasingly elaborate expertise to even understand.

Americans despise lawyers and love judicial review. But they cannot have it both ways. They cannot insist that a judicial oligarchy, or even aristocracy, not speak the dialect of the law. They cannot insist that a complex apparatus of graduated political and legal elites, culminating in a paramount constitutional elite, represents a "democracy" that, somehow, has fallen into the hands of the legal profession. They equally cannot insist that all of this is constitutional. What the American system is, in fact, is a judicially dominated unitary structure, wherein the will of the judges rules, but wherein it finds articulation as the will of the sovereign people.

Such is the form. The reality is a concentration of authority and a uniformity of control which accompanies the centralizing power that attends an emerging order of corporate feudalism or, more accurately, dynasty, and no institution is more suited to govern this reality than that which is predicated on the traditional principle of aristocracy, an institution which attains a politically necessary consent by expressing itself in the permutations of popular sovereignty. Here is a central clue to the dominance of judicial review, and to the forces behind its successful subversion of what, for a short time, was a constitutional republic.

Notes

1. Jerrold K. Footlick, With Bureau Reports, "Too Much Law?," *Newsweek*, January 10, 1977, p. 43.

2. Arthur E. Sutherland, *Constitutionalism in America: Origin and Evolution of Its Fundamental Ideas* (New York: Blaisdell Publishing Co., 1965), pp. 3, 43.

3. Mauro Cappelletti, *Judicial Review in the Contemporary World* (Indianapolis: The Bobbs-Merrill Co., 1971), p. 1.

American Democracy

The Crucial Contradiction

(1978)

The Problem

Within the first years of the twentieth century, the law of chronic depression was discovered. Formulated by Karl Kautsky, it identified the crucial contradiction of capitalism as the buildup of venture capital with no place to go. Short of a redistribution of wealth, and of the instruments of wealth production, measures which would totally unsettle the established power arrangements, the order would choke on an oversupply of precisely that which it produced best—profits to be returned to wealth production in the form of investment capital.

The revolutionary implications of the law of chronic depression were lost on many who would make the revolution, but not on the great capital interests. By the middle of the century, liberal politicians in America had devised what appeared to be a permanent solution—the "war-preparations economy."[1] Through this apparatus, capital seeking investment found a guaranteed outlet in the planned obsolescence of military production; found it in magnitudes proportionate to the size of the capital-surplus problem; and found it with an affiliated certainty of a handsome profit. While the genius of the system was little appreciated by the people, the central feature of its operation subtly became the foundation of public life in the United States. Indeed, so subtle was its intrusion that for many years most economists failed to recognize its existence.

Avoided were the uncertainties of augmenting domestic demand, with its cycles of boom and bust, its periodic crises, and its associated need to encourage consumption as opposed to investment. Also—and most important—avoided were the social and political pitfalls of putting more money into people's hands, a policy which contained the insidious tendency of enhancing the liberty, status, and power of the general population in relation to those who ruled. What was needed were assured buyers, and no disruption of the systemic relationships which, in the final analysis, were what capitalist economics was all about. For this purpose, continual preparation for a war that, ideally, never took place was perfect. The purchasing ability of the population could be stabilized or reduced. Production for military use was inordinately expensive and immediately out of date. The suzerainty of the aristocracy of capital was automatically preserved.

Helpfully, the aggregates of dollars involved were beyond the comprehension of most human beings. Conceiving of billions is much like conceiving of light years—the necessary abstractions are elusive and difficult to relate to what appears tangible, at least for those not expert in such matters. A slight increase in warfare spending could easily, and without public notice, more than compensate concentrated capital for the traditional fluctuations of domestic markets. Untoward effects on profitability could be managed out of existence.

By the 1970's, none of this was new. But what suddenly appeared as possibly new was that the American people might begin to grasp the corporate realities of an economic system they preferred to think of as "free enterprise." This danger, as is well known, was long controlled by a sophisticated barrage of anti-Communist propaganda which transformed thinking too hard about the actualities of the American economy into treason.

Yet the military excesses of a nonwar in Indochina, capped—as it turned out—in the national mind by the Watergate episode and its attendant revelations, induced an un-American cynicism into a normally optimistic population. Elements, particularly among the young, became resistant to the erasure-like assurances of the mandarins who served power. Even worse, they grew more overtly restive in regard to the general inequities that characterized the order. Although a minority, they represented an edge of skepticism, and an emerging concern to those in power. This concern intensified during the Great Oil Boycott of 1973-1974, when too many people began placing blame for high fuel prices on the international oil companies instead of on "foreigners" cast by the merchandisers of consent[2] into the role of culprits.

About this time an interesting fact about the American outlook was noted, and much commented on in ruling circles. A substantial augmentation of federal spending for military procurement and research in an amount necessary to compensate the capital interests for slumping automobile sales was hardly noticed by anyone. Such augmentations had become so normal they were simply accepted as part of the proper functioning of the system. They were good for business, and the labor movement and progressive Congressmen had become deeply accustomed to viewing them as the most acceptable technique of enhancing employment opportunities. If an industry so central to the economy, and so visible to popular perception, could be so easily rescued, the possibilities were great indeed. The inferences of this line of thought were not long in becoming manifest.

It was generally understood that the war-preparations budget, which provided an assured market at an assured price, plus cost over-runs to enhance profitability, was well suited to the corporate need for long-range planning and a highly expensive structure of research and development. Now the remaining uncertainties of capitalism could finally be dissolved. The problem of economic depression could be eradicated, and the inconveniences of pricing at marketable levels, sales promotion, advertising, recessions, and the political effects of a corporate inflation could be dispensed with. All of this, it was finally perceived, could be accomplished through war production alone. The idea was simple, and possessed great appeal to the liberal desire for symmetrical arrangement. If the military budget was sufficiently expanded, a consumer market would not be necessary at all.

True, the annoying demands of those engaged in war production still had to be attended to, and they, unfortunately, comprised a market. But this proved to be a temporary phase. Liberal thought is invariably circular. Corresponding to the new realization that "capitalism" no longer required human beings because it no longer required markets, was the development of a technology which made a total automation of production possible. Provided the proper federal funding by "business"-oriented administrations—funding well hidden within the overall military budget—this became an operational reality. Of course, given the economic sophistication of the American people, what they were not told by mass media they would not know, and few realized that the new policy was rendering them obsolete as a financial necessity. Those who did realize were not heard.

Thus it came to be that workers were replaced by technological innovation while the traditional capitalist markets dissolved into the only necessary "market," the market of war production. There were, undoubtedly, still substantial nonmilitary possibilities for the transfer of capital overseas. The policy of detente, for instance, provided large and emerging markets for investment in the Soviet Union and China, but not at the rate of return which had been customary in the eras of colonialism and imperialism, and certainly not at the rate guaranteed by manufacturing for military use. These investments were useful but, clearly, not useful enough. At first, there was a crude effort to improve the position of the United States as the paramount armaments exporter to the world. As the former colonies of the Western powers broke loose, and began to sell raw materials at higher prices, it was felt that the sale of weapons to these countries would strengthen the dollar in international money markets and improve the capitalization picture at home, allowing the innovation relevant to the American military position in the world, and ensuring that what was already available would be adequately obsolete.

There had, of course, long existed a program to extend military purchasing credits to other countries for this exact purpose, as well as to allow the "leaders" of these countries to maintain control over their own people and, incidentally, to preserve a welcome situation for American investment dollars—a program euphemistically known as "foreign aid." This continued for a time, although it gradually dissipated and eventually expired. The resultant slack in foreign demand for military hardware was more than compensated for by the purchases of the newly-rich oil countries and other former colonial exporters of raw materials vital to war production. But, in the long run, these countries became sufficiently industrialized through the profitable exportation of American technological expertise to develop their own armaments industries. As a consequence, a policy that intensified the rate at which military hardware was declared outmoded became mandated.

New weapons were now necessary each year purely to maintain parity with the innovations possible in such weapons, innovations most certainly in the possession of the "other side." Yet, as people were phased out of the economy, the need to rationalize economic policy in terms of foreign policy weakened. Gradually, the identity of the other side became vague, finally to disappear as an unnecessary complication. Obsolescence had replaced sales to foreign countries. Now it replaced "national defense" itself.

Unfettered by the political inconvenience of inhabitants, the system was freed. Prices lost all semblance of relationship to domestic demand. The arms budget soared. The production of advanced weapons could fully keep pace with the technical possibilities of what could be produced, as well as with the pressures of an enormous aggregate of investment capital generated by an enormous magnification of governmental buying.

Among those who ruled were some who found relief in finally admitting to others—and to themselves—what "capitalist" opportunity was really about.

The Solution

What happened to those who previously occupied the United States is not fully understood. Nevertheless the outlines are known. It is documented that, for a time, substantial numbers of people survived through a reversion to berry picking and the hunting of previously domesticated animals which, in turn, decreased the human population by hunting them. This ended when the conglomerate reach of war industries bought all the land in the country to engage in the highly profitable enterprise of food production for military use. From then on, the tactics of survival could only take place on an illegal basis. Such was the American respect for the rights of the propertied—and of property—that multitudes willingly evaporated rather than trespass on posted land. It is not known how many put to sea, where they were driven beyond the twelve-mile limit by the fact of oil-company control of coastal waters, never to be heard from again.

There is serious speculation that the final solution to the population problem was not achieved through the natural laws of laissez faire, but by the application of chemical sprays from military aircraft as part of a Pentagon testing program. This spray apparently conditioned those whose social upbringing was improper to a deep regard for ownership and a legitimate return on dollar investment. There was a further guarantee that official policy would be respected. The conditioning induced by the spray was chemically inherited by any children that might be born, ensuring that the need to disappear in the name of property rights would be permanent.

Others suggest that the people were dramatically and largely eliminated when a small proportion of the existing armaments was turned on them. But such gross action implies that the right wing had taken total control of the government, an improbability in a country which was fundamentally committed to a progressive liberalism. It is more likely that years of socialization to the propaganda of the warfare state remained sufficiently effective to induce most of those who were left to remove themselves as a patriotic gesture.

All of this is conjecture. The details may never be known. What is patent, however, is that the American population, which had come to represent a political impediment to a rational economic program, declined, and only those required by the imperatives of military technology remained. Becoming unnecessary to corporate capital, the masses withered away in a great reversal of historical prediction. Thus did Yankee ingenuity triumph over the Germanic scribblings of Karl Marx.

When it came about that no people were required and, hence, none remained, is not entirely clear. It is, of course, well documented that the computer came to do all the design, planning, and tooling associated with manufacturing and, undoubtedly, could have handled the sales promotion for which there was no longer any need. There is, moreover, no question that one generation of computers was able to create a new one capable of even greater sophistication than its predecessors. Some surmise that a variety of minor wars was engaged in by these computers in order to experiment with the weapons produced and, as they increasingly adopted arcane human characteristics, to assure themselves that what they produced was necessary. Although unproven, it is likely that the rulers of the order were the victims of one or more of these experimental operations while computers, considered truly pivotal to the system, were by this time constructed to withstand such assaults.

These matters will probably never be comprehended with certainty because the political simplicity of the emerging economics had obvious appeal to insecure leaders all over the globe and, as the nations of the world adopted the American approach to production, they, too, ran out of people. Yet the problems of investment opportunities for venture capital were greatly eased, and the American revolution was finally complete. As Jefferson had advocated, the experience of the United States became the model for the world.

Eventually there was no one around to ponder whatever wisdom a study of these events might afford. Indeed, there was no one to gather the facts. This is why knowledge of this period is so vague. Even this is not really known because there is no one available to really know it. All that can be said is that the logic of corporate "democracy" at last fulfilled itself, and there is universal agreement that logic is a consideration which cannot be ignored.

Notes

1. The earliest usage of this term is found in Paul M. Sweezy, "The American Economy and the Threat of War," *Monthly Review*, November, 1950, p. 340.

2. With apologies to Robert Bendiner, "The 'Engineering of Consent'—A Case Study," *The Reporter*, August 14, 1955, pp. 14-23.

Theft as the Basis of American Public Policy

An Instructive Instance

(1985)

Americans, in their central perceptions of themselves, are "earners." We are a people who believe in the work ethic, in "deserving" what we get.

Yet few Americans realize that this decisive element of their ideology derives from something called "the labor theory of value." This is an idea not invented by Karl Marx, who hurled it against those who did invent it. In its developed sense, it is a creation of certain seventeenth-century British writers, such as James Harrington and John Locke, who advocate an economic system eventually known as "capitalism." The labor theory of value is subsequently employed by Adam Smith, Robert Malthus, and David Ricardo who, along with Jeremy Bentham, James Mill, and John Stuart Mill, propound the essential postulates of what becomes the capitalist tradition.

There are two elements which, when taken together, comprise the labor theory of value. First is the conviction that material wealth—what economists formulate as goods and services—results from the application of human labor, physical or mental or both, to natural resources. The second element, although it reasonably follows from the first, is not "theoretical" at all. It does not attempt to explain anything. It is doctrinal and moral, advancing the idea that people possess a legitimate claim on wealth only in exact proportion to the amount of labor, including the training necessary for this labor, that they previously expended in the actual production of the wealth. Herein is the argument for "earning."

The labor theory of value is, historically, a capitalist reaction against the arrangements of financial privilege which prevail in

Europe during the ages of feudalism and dynasty. With this centrally in mind, Locke contends that "the earth and all that is therein is given to men for the support and comfort of their being," and that these "belong to mankind in common, as they are produced by the spontaneous hand of nature; and nobody has originally a private dominion exclusive of the rest of mankind in any of them."[1]

Hence a claim to wealth must be predicated on the fact that every human being "has a property in his own person" in accord with the laws of nature, and "whatsoever then he removes out of the state that nature has provided and left it in, he has mixed his labor with, and joined it to something that is his own, and thereby makes it his property." In short, it is only through "the labor of his body and the work of his hands"[2] that any individual realizes a "right" to ownership of private wealth.

To reiterate, the labor theory of value is not only a theory; it is also a doctrine of entitlement which is intended to subvert the foundation of an order constructed upon a presumptive ownership of natural resources, a doctrine which contends that no one is allowed a claim on natural resources without mixing their labor with them. It assaults a system that affirms the propriety of wealth rooted in the power and inherited privilege of royalty, along with its surrogates and sycophantic extensions.

This does not change, as is often argued, with Locke's further description of the invention of money. Money allows surplus wealth to be stored up for future exchange for use value. It does not touch the question of how this wealth is to be acquired, and is certainly not inconsistent with a position which insists that income must be proportionate to labor expended. To allege that money justifies the accumulation of wealth through the exploitation of the labor of others is to suggest that Locke was a feeble logician. This is possible. But it is more likely that such an interpretation is less reflective of what Locke actually wrote than it is of a need to use Locke to rationalize that which exists.

Logic notwithstanding, the labor theory of value comes to America in the heads of those who compose the great English immigrations to North America in the eighteenth century. Every society is held together by controlling agreements as to why things are the way they are. Central to these agreements is a need for a morally acceptable explanation of why the financial condition of each is not equal. This is a pervasive political reality. It demands a definition of the relative economic "worth" of human beings. In this sense, the labor theory of value is critical to what will become American ideology.

But, after Locke, an additional element is introduced into capitalist thought. Economic writers begin to entertain the idea that among those rights which derive from natural law is not only the right to property, but a right to the fruits that property itself might yield. This becomes an entrepreneurial right which permits a command on wealth that exceeds recovery of the total cost of doing business. To some this is known as "surplus value." Others simply refer to it as "profit."

If wealth is produced by labor, and if some make a successful claim to wealth which surpasses the total cost of production, including their own labor, this extra wealth must come from somewhere. Given the labor theory of value, it must come from labor. Certainly, if those who demand profit obtain it, those who create the wealth which profit represents cannot receive the whole value of the wealth they create. To the degree that this is the case, those who do not labor get, and those who do labor do not.

This is a blatant violation of the doctrine of entitlement within the labor theory of value, a doctrine which the advocates of profit allegedly admire, and which consolidates the economic order. It is on this basis that Marx refers to profit as theft, a "right" to wealth stolen from those who work to produce it and, if they work in their own business, from themselves.

Such a conclusion is logically necessary. Even establishment economists refer to profit as "unearned increment." And, while most Western economic thinkers do not like the labor theory of value because, ostensibly, it fails to explain reality, they are yet to replace its embarrassing doctrinal consequences with a formulation which rationalizes the actualities of wealth distribution. They have not replaced it because they cannot. The result is a logical contradiction which pervades capitalism after the British seventeenth century, a contradiction which even Ricardo, try as he will, is unable to resolve. Plainly, the labor theory of value and the right to profit are at war, a feature of capitalism which produces a continual tension that becomes manifest in the political reflections of its economic system.

All of which brings us back to America. No people in the world love "capitalism" more. We are enamored of both earning and profit.

It follows that most Americans perceive those on welfare as basically despicable for not "earning" their own way, to the point where many agree with the Social Darwinists who propose that such people should not be assisted in surviving and reproducing their own "inferior" type. Yet it also follows that Americans defer to those who grow rich on unearned increment. Indeed, these are persons who are characteristically emulated. While applauding the industrious for their contributions to production, the real penchant of most Americans is to never work again, and to become wealthy through investments while not doing anything more productive than consume. What results is a nation of alienated labor which profoundly admires doing nothing—provided, of course, that those who do nothing get rich while doing it.

Herein revealed is a persistent American desire to steal wealth from those who produce it and who, according to the labor theory of value, are entitled to it. Thus expressed is an "ambition" which permeates the existence of those who actually work as well as those who do not. It is an implicit tribute to the power of the capitalist idea within an oligopolistic order which is demonstrably not capitalistic and, in particular, to the contention for profit within that idea.

This cannot be a matter of human nature. Too much evidence of other contemporary systemic attitudes and of other historical times mitigate against this possibility. It is really a matter of a dominant national ideology which characterizes the United States and the much-applauded arrival of "the people's capitalism."

A few years ago, this was impressively articulated during the great political furor regarding a federal withholding tax on dividend payments. Here, it will be recalled, was the price that the Reagan administration paid to get the more progressive members of Congress to go along with a tax increase which was suddenly deemed necessary to reduce the deficits and unemployment that devolved from the tax cuts for the corporate rich which rendered the administration famous. The feeling among some in Congress was that those who most benefitted from the tax reductions ought to give a little of it back.

Hence a withholding tax on dividends, making it a bit more difficult for the recipients of corporate profits to cheat on reported income while the immediate cash on hand available to the federal government was symmetrically augmented. A withholding tax long applied to wages and salaries. It was deemed fair to apply it to dividends as well.

Surprisingly, the President "supported" the bill, which quickly became law. Soon, however, the pressure began. The sentiment in Congress was reversed and, after a short time, so was the vote on the measure. A bill repealing the withholding tax on dividends was sent to the White House. The President huffed and he puffed. He even threatened to veto the repeal. Then he quietly signed it with, needless to say, little publicity and fanfare. Few souvenir pens were handed out that day to the appropriately august members of Congress. In fact, none may have been handed out at all.

What is of interest is not that the banking industry, and those it could gull into acting as its surrogates, carried out an intensive, misleading, and successful campaign to get the original policy rescinded. This was nothing new in the "commercial republic," although the media attention it attracted was unusual. What is of interest is the ideological substance of that campaign and the notable absence of resistance to the repeal within either of the major political parties. Certainly, the power of "the financial community," a euphemism which suggests that only its members, whoever they are, possess any intelligent concern about money, is a phenomenon worthy of careful consideration.

It is accepted that dividends are payments of interest on money invested and that, in the proportion that a person's income is based on interest, they comprise a command on wealth by someone who did not work for it and who, therefore, did not produce it. This is because interest, by traditional definition, is profit. It results from the employment of venture capital, a profit "earned" from what Brandeis cogently refers to as "other people's money,"[3] becoming a claim on wealth attained through the investment of the money of someone else.

The capital that is so invested, and that makes dividends possible, must be already expended labor in an accumulated form because, compatible with the labor theory of value, wealth, of which capital is a representation, can only be created by the application of labor units to natural resources. This is labor that cannot be completely paid for, otherwise there would be no profit and, under the present system, very little capital to invest. For workers to translate a percentage of their wages or salaries into socially significant investment would probably mean that they would have to receive the actual productive value of their labor, a possibility that is fundamentally subversive to the ongoing national arrangement. As it is now, it is profit, or unearned increment, which yields the great preponderance of venture capital in America.

All of this is compatible with classical capitalist economic exposition. It also leads to the conclusion that venture capital in the United States is almost entirely derived from theft, whether perpetrated by the "public sector," in the form of the state, or by the "private sector," in the form of business enterprise. Given the labor theory of value, no other conclusion is possible. If, in the face of this conclusion, the labor theory of value is discarded, then some other justification of why wealth is not equally distributed must be invented if theft is not to become legal and if society is not to tear itself apart. But, having escaped the earlier formulation that gold is value, no important capitalist writer really attempts to dismiss the labor theory of value. As a result, a people deeply conditioned to capitalist ideas continue to be committed to the logical inferences of its formulation to and the disconcerting contradiction between earning and profit.

In this regard, one has to deal with athletes and other entertainers whose "salaries" result not from attendance but from television contracts which reflect the profitability rates of the corporate sponsors of almost all mass media events in the United States. These "salaries" are really investments and, as such, articulate the "proper" employment of venture capital. Yet not all profit becomes venture capital. Some is simply spent on the much-admired opulence of those who are, supposedly, most crucial to material production. Some is also absorbed by the consumption patterns of a working class which only knows itself as "the middle class" and which, moreover, emulates the investment behavior of those who are richer and, thereby, more "worthy." Nevertheless, the issue of who creates wealth, and who is entitled to it and in what amount, remains a fundamental American preoccupation. This is because, at bottom, the labor theory of value continues to be an American embarrassment.

The repeal of a withholding tax on dividends patently proclaims the public policy of the United States. To the extent that people work for a living, a part of what they earn may be withheld by various governments at, it should be noted, no interest. But, to the extent that an income is derived from not working, those who are "employed" in this manner must be able to protect what they "earn" and not have their "earnings" interrupted by a tax which represents a "public" intrusion into their "private" affairs. Undoubtedly, these people are of a superior type and are more to be trusted to pay their taxes than those who merely work. Any mix of income must be treated with a respect for this understanding. Indeed, within the inherent demands of an ideology which loves the earner but which loves profit more, this is only reasonable. What it reflects is the reality of the American dream, the desire, as Veblen pointed out long ago, for an ideal condition wherein people, in a society that admires material acquisition, receive the status that attains to those who possess enormous wealth and who are engaged in doing absolutely nothing to create it.

This ideal condition is also known as "incentive" which, in American terms, means the "right" to no longer earn but to steal. Such is the consciousness of a nation wherein profit is "earned" and not defined as theft; wherein the paid leisure of the wealthy is not considered welfare; and wherein a middle class which is actually a working class perceives its financial interests as compatible with those of the anointed rich who do not need to work.

Plainly, the world is "wealthy" in an absence of logic and moral consistency. So it is to be expected that the market of earners advocated by the early capitalists is transformed into an economy in which profitability, increasingly corporate in character, becomes the order of the day. It can also be expected that very few are aware of the surrender of labor to theft. In this world, complaint can come only from those who fail to steal "enough" and who, accordingly, envy those who do. Of course, if the few persistently control more of the wealth, those who actually produce it get less proportionate to their production. The battle over a withholding tax on dividends should suggest that a certain degree of hypocritical deploring is necessary in America. But it might be refreshing if we stopped acting surprised.

Notes

1. John Locke, *The Second Treatise of Government*, ed. with an intro. by Thomas P. Reardon, The Library of Liberal Arts (Indianapolis: The Bobbs-Merrill Co., 1952), p. 17.

2. Ibid.

3. Louis D. Brandeis, *Other People's Money: And How the Bankers Use It*, with a Foreword by Norman Hapgood (New York: Frederick A. Stokes, Co., 1932).

The House of Forty Thieves

Or the Limits of Equal Opportunity

(1983)

The House of Forty Thieves

As is well known among those who are not themselves thieves or, at least, do not perceive themselves as thieves, honor is a paramount trait of persons who pursue the contours of this profession. Thus did honor saturate a gray building full of dingy printer's offices and inky shops on Prince Street in the lower part of Manhattan Island in the halcyon days of what is now known as the Great Depression. The place was a rat's nest, a honeycomb, a labyrinth of cubbyholes and a variety of types who in one way or another seemed human. What they shared was distrust. They revealed to none, and only the initiated could comprehend them, these unwashed from beyond the frontiers of what was understood to be civilization.

Within the maze of offices and shops there were forty cubicles, forty places to defend against any who would wrest away the security of established ground. At the time spoken of here, all were filled. This story only can be told because on a March day of scudding low clouds and the threat of a grimy rain, the forty-first applicant appeared.

The man was harried, worried looking, some would say desperate in countenance except, in the time of its happening, so many looked that way that few noticed anymore. There were, of course, no places. Not a cubbyhole, not a rat's nest, not a cubicle in the entire network which loomed above the alcove of the rental agent. But the man was insistent. There must be something. He had tried all of Prince Street, he could not afford the rent anywhere else and, in any event, the street was devoid of a vacancy. Without a cubicle he could not pursue his ambition, he could not print the cards, leaflets, and circulars that were the produce of his creative applications; in short, he needed a cubicle if he was to be a thief.

Since the applicant and the agent had meandered out into the lobby while this fervent appeal was issued, what was said fell upon the ears of one of the resident thieves taking his leave of the labyrinth as he set out to discover fresh directions for his talents. As has been said, there is honor among thieves, especially at a price. The price was soon settled, and that afternoon the forty-first applicant found his place within a niche of a cubicle, free, at a fee, to use the presses and other necessary equipment of the proprietor with the alert ears.

When residing in a den full of thieves, one must understand that a deal is a deal unless it can be broken to the advantage of whoever perceives momentary leverage. Accordingly, the rent went up, the thief with the ears claiming that the applicant had not understood that the proprietor was entitled to a percentage of any work taken in by the applicant, who was also to pay a portion of the utilities equal to one-half of the total bill each month. Such income depletion was not possible, and the applicant began to knock on the door of cubicle after cubicle in an attempt to secure a more advantageous and stable arrangement. There was much interest in his proposal, and he moved what had to be moved to a cubbyhole three floors above his first niche. Still the result was the same, since there is honor not only among some thieves, but among all. After six of these moves, the applicant was discouraged, yet the thought of departing the security of a Prince Street address was too intolerable to bear.

Matters were made worse by the honorable practice of undercutting on a job. A quick telephone call to the customer by the proprietor of whatever niche the applicant currently occupied more often than not would result in the transfer of an order, usually without the knowledge of the applicant who, upon the presentation of his finished work, was informed by the customer that his "partner" had offered a new price and was handling the matter. Hence did the applicant learn the value of secrecy, a condition difficult to achieve since he was never in a position to operate behind closed doors.

Earnestly he petitioned the rental agent for a rat's nest of his own, merely to be informed that the resident thieves were stable in their geographic claims. The result was inevitable. The applicant was forced to leave his Prince Street home. He finally did so, grudgingly, knowing he was in an ideal location to ply his trade, yet realizing that honor among thieves dictates room only for a finite membership in the fraternity of practitioners of this noble and respected profession.

Notes